VICTORIAN BRITAIN

Contents

Introduction

Have you ever been to London? You may have travelled to Victoria station or visited the Victoria and Albert Museum. These are named after Queen Victoria and her husband Prince Albert.

Victoria was crowned queen of England in 1837, when she was just 18 years old. When she was 21 she married a German called Albert. Prince Albert was known as the Prince Consort. He took a great interest in British affairs, science, technology, and in working conditions.

Queen Victoria is one of the most famous of all British monarchs. She ruled for 64 years. During her reign Britain became the richest and most powerful country in the world. Many people had not liked the last two kings, but when Queen Victoria died, millions of people were sad.

▲ *Painting of Queen Victoria, Prince Albert, and some of their children.*

LOOKING AT EVIDENCE

There is plenty of evidence that tells us about life in Victorian Britain – and it is all around us!

▲ *Victorian schools had separate entrances for boys and girls because they were taught separately. We can still see these entrances at schools built in Victorian times, but we don't use them now.*

▲ *There may be Victorian houses, schools or factories near where you live. This building was a cotton mill in Victorian times.*

Times of change

Victoria and Albert had a great influence on the people of Britain. The Victorian period was a time of great change. New inventions changed the way people lived. New ideas changed the way people thought about the world. Here are just some of the exciting things that happened during Victoria's reign:

- Electricity was used for lights.
- The train replaced the stage-coach.
- The car was invented.
- All men were allowed to vote.
- Children from all families could go to school.
- Working conditions were improved, especially for women and children.
- Child labour in factories and mines was stopped.
- The Christmas tree was introduced to Britain by Prince Albert.
- Photography was invented.
- Britain gained a large empire.

▲ *Have you ever seen the letters 'VR' on a letterbox near where you live? 'Victoria Regina' is Latin for Queen Victoria.*

Victorian towns

The growth of towns

During Victoria's reign cities and towns in Britain grew and grew. Small villages that had once been out in the country became part of the spreading cities. Villages like Westminster, Kensington and Camberwell became part of London. In 1801 there were fewer than one million people living in London. By the end of Victoria's reign in 1901 there were over four million people living in London.

Other areas also grew rapidly, especially the industrial areas of the north-west of England including Lancashire and Cheshire, Teesside, South Wales, Whitehaven in Cumbria, and Birmingham. During the 19th century (1800–1900) the population of Birmingham grew from 70,000 to over half a million (500,000). Manchester grew from 80,000 to over 860,000.

Nearly all this growth went on without any town planning. Cheap terraced houses were built next to smoky factories. Town life was not very pleasant!

In Victorian times towns and cities in Britain grew much bigger. There were many reasons for this:

- During Victorian times many large factories were built. The owners needed lots of people to work in the factories.

- There was an increase in the population.

- There were fewer jobs in the country. People from the country crowded into the towns and cities looking for work.

- People also came from Scotland and Ireland, and large numbers came from the rest of Europe.

These maps show the main population areas in Britain before (left) and after Victorian times (right). The keys show the population per square kilometre.

OVER 100

OVER 3000

OVER 1500

◀ Manchester looked like this in the 1860s. Notice all the chimneys and the smoke-filled air.

▼ The Victorians built many elegant city squares, like this one in Belgravia in London. The houses here were the city homes of some of the richest families in Britain. These people would often have their own country homes as well.

Town life for the wealthy

The wealthier middle and upper classes moved away from the factories. They usually tried to live to the west of the main town so that the wind would blow the smell and smoke away from them. Their homes were elegant and their streets were properly paved. Private parks were often created nearby.

▲ Seaside resort towns grew as rail fares became cheaper. Even poor people could afford a day trip.

Small towns

By the end of the century (1900) large numbers of wealthy people lived outside the main cities in smaller towns. The spread of the railways helped them to travel to and from the cities.

Some towns like Torquay, Buxton and Scarborough grew up as places of leisure for those city dwellers who could afford the train fare and the hotel bill. Places like Blackpool and Margate became famous for day trips.

The city slums

Life in parts of the big towns and cities was terrible. The streets were crowded, busy and dirty. There were often no underground sewers, so sewage was often left to find its own way slowly into a nearby river. No one cleared the rubbish, and it was left to rot in the streets.

The poor workers lived close to the factories in small overcrowded houses. Whole families often shared a single room. The air was thick with smoke and soot from the factories. Water had to be collected from a pump in the street which was shared by many houses. This water was often polluted. Life was so unhealthy that only about seven children out of every ten would live to become adults.

▲ *In Victorian slum streets there was often only one standpipe for water which was shared by the neighbourhood and was turned on for 20 minutes a day.*

POINTS OF VIEW

Many children stole things so that they could eat. Do you think they should have broken the law like this?

Children who lived on the streets were called 'Street Arabs'. No one looked after them or fed them. They slept in doorways and often went for days without eating.

Street children

City streets were full of homeless people. Many of them were orphans. Some lived in the local workhouse where they were often separated from their parents. Conditions were poor but a little better than being on the streets.

Charles Dickens wrote about the lives of poor Victorian children in his book *Oliver Twist*. Oliver has to work in a workhouse. When he meets an orphan called the Artful Dodger, he learns how to be a pickpocket. Many street children had to steal or beg for their food.

Help for the poor

Many Victorians did their best to help the poor. Dr Barnardo opened a home for orphaned children in London. William Booth founded the Salvation Army to care for the homeless and poor.

Gradually some improvements were made, but it was not until 1848 that Parliament passed laws to make towns and cities cleaner and healthier places. City councils began to clean up the slums. Proper sewers and drains were built. These improvements helped people live healthier, longer lives.

▶ Dr Barnardo established homes for Victorian street children. Many Barnardo homes for orphans still exist today.

Shops and shopping

People who lived in towns and cities did not grow their own food; they had to buy it. Poor people often bought their food at local markets, but gradually shops became more important.

Shops were usually small family businesses, often specialising in a few items. They often provided their own delivery services to wealthier families. Delivery boys and tradesmen would call for orders in the morning and would deliver the items an hour or so later. A middle-class housewife could do most of her everyday shopping without leaving the home!

▲ *Goods displayed outside a gentlemen's clothes shop.*

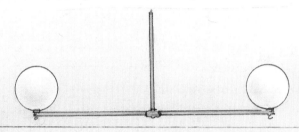

Street traders

Street traders would tour the streets and alleys shouting out their calls to attract customers. Almost anything could be bought in the street. Young boys would even clean your shoes.

The towns would also have other people working in the street, lighting the lamps or sweeping up after horses.

1. This muffin seller is ringing a bell to attract customers.

2. There were many flower sellers in cities like London.

3. Each night the gas lamplighter would have to go around every lamp-post to light the gas.

Department and chain stores

Gradually some shops in the bigger towns grew into larger stores. The first department store was William Whiteley's 'The Universal Provider'. Many shop assistants worked in these department stores, selling all sorts of goods. Some shop owners did so well that they opened shops in other towns and so created what we call 'chain stores'. Jesse Boot started a chemist's shop in Nottingham and W H Smith began with newspaper stalls on railway stations. These chain stores are now in most towns.

Victorian houses

Houses for the poor

Poor factory workers lived in small back-to-back houses, close to the factories where they worked. Some of these houses had narrow alleyways between them, while others really did join each other at the back. Most of them had one or two rooms downstairs and one or two rooms upstairs. Although the houses were small many Victorian families were big, with four or five children. Some of the poorest families had to share houses, so that a whole family would have to live in only one room.

Towards the end of the Victorian period this sort of housing improved. Houses were built with their own water supply and their own toilet. The toilet was usually outside in the yard.

In one street there is only one toilet for 380 inhabitants.

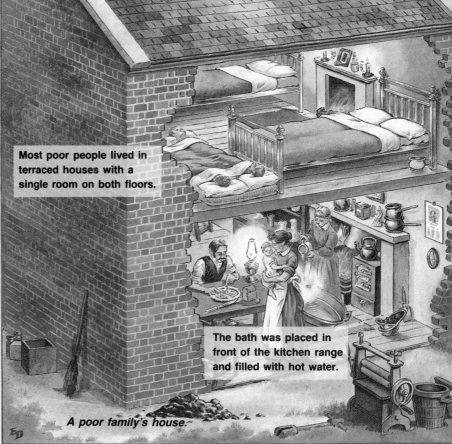

Most poor people lived in terraced houses with a single room on both floors.

The bath was placed in front of the kitchen range and filled with hot water.

A poor family's house.

Houses for the rich

The middle and upper classes had much better housing. Some were terraced, some were detached or semi-detached. These homes were filled with large furniture. The wealthier families would have had all the latest gadgets like gas-heated baths or mangles. Every room had a coal fireplace for heating.

Many of the worst Victorian slums have been demolished but there are still many other Victorian houses in towns and cities today.

◀ *In Victorian times these houses would only have had one pump to supply all their water. The sewer would have run down the middle of the street.*

▼ *A rich family's house. You can see that it is quite a modern house with toilets and a bathroom, but do you know what a scullery, drawing room and pantry are?*

Cook's bedroom

Parlourmaid's and housemaid's bedroom

Governess's bedroom

Children's bedroom

Nursery

Study

Bathroom

Parents' bedroom

Dining room

Drawing room

Scullery

Pantry

Kitchen

Rich families

In Victorian times people who owned land or factories, or had important jobs, became very rich. They had enough money to afford a good education for their children and to buy beautiful furniture to decorate their large houses. The pictures on this page show what the inside of some of their houses would have been like. They are beautifully furnished with large, well-made furniture, often rather dark in colour. The wallpaper and paint were dark too; this was to hide all the dirt of everyday Victorian life.

The head of the Victorian household was the father. He was often stern and quite strict with his wife and children. His wife was in charge of the servants and the running of the household, though she would not do any of the housework or cooking herself.

▲ A Victorian family photograph, taken in 1890.

◀ A <u>reconstruction</u>, in a museum, of a Victorian drawing room. See how cluttered the room is.

▶ A group of 12 servants in front of a late Victorian house.

Many middle-class children saw little of their parents. They were often brought up in the nursery by a nanny. As they grew older they might be sent to school or have a tutor or governess to teach them at home.

▲ *A reconstruction of a nursery in a rich Victorian's house.*

Servants

In these homes there would have been a number of servants to clean and cook. The servants worked long hours, often rising at 4 a.m. and working through until 10 p.m. Much of the time would be spent carrying coal from the coal shed to the various rooms in the house to keep the house warm.

Poor families

Families with incomes or jobs had enough money to buy or rent small terraced houses. Life for them gradually improved during Victoria's reign. There were improvements in working conditions in the factories, in their pay, and in health and education.

Father, and often Mother, would work. The mother would also have to work very hard in the home. She had to feed her family and keep them looking clean and tidy with no modern equipment like washing machines or electric irons. In the early part of the century some of the children might also have gone out to work, but later children went to the local school.

▶ *Many homes also acted as workshops. The mother and children stayed at home and did work like dressmaking, or they may have taken in other people's laundry. This family earned money at their home in the East End of London by making matchboxes.*

> I live with my three daughters, son and our two lodgers. We have two beds to share between us.

Some families were much poorer. They had to live in small rooms, perhaps in a cellar or attic. Many could not afford to buy new furniture or clothes. Clothes were sold in second-hand shops or handed down from one child to the next. Children often had to wear clothes that were far too big or small for them.

Poor families could only afford to buy very simple food. Most of the time they ate porridge, bread, milk and potatoes. Meat or eggs were a special treat.

Food in the workhouse was terrible. Inmates were often fed only on a thin porridge called gruel. They had to eat in silence.

Life in the workhouse

The poorest of all families were those that had to live in the workhouse. In the workhouse men, women and children were split up and had to work and sleep in different rooms, even if they were from the same family! Everyone had to wear workhouse clothes and obey workhouse laws. They had to do hard work, like chopping wood or breaking up stones for road building, and were punished if they did not work hard enough.

POINTS OF VIEW

Many Victorians thought that poor people were lazy. They made life in the workhouses very unpleasant to stop others wanting to go there. Other Victorians thought the poor should be helped more.
What do you think?

Factories and mines

A long day in the factory

Many new factories were built during Victoria's reign. The factory owners employed a lot of workers, but they paid them very little money and made them work long hours. They wanted their expensive new machines to run all day long, only stopping for major repairs. In this way the factory owners could make many products for very little money. Much of the production was then exported, and the factory owners made large profits.

The workers' lives were miserable. They had to get up at dawn and returned home exhausted at night. They had to work for 12 or 14 hours a day with very few breaks. Their work was boring and dangerous. There were no guards or fences around the machines to prevent accidents from happening.

The workers dared not complain. There were plenty of unemployed people who would take their jobs if they were sacked.

▲ This is a textile mill. Look for the drive belts. These big machines were able to drive a lot of smaller machines. The factory would have been very noisy and full of cotton dust.

Female 'drawers' pulled coal out of the mines with a chain attached to a belt around their waist.

A hard day in the mines

This is sore, sore work. I wish to God the first woman who tried to bear coals had broken her back and none would have tried it again.

Coal was a vital ingredient of Victorian life. It provided heat for the home and for cooking but more importantly it was the fuel for the factories and railways. Britain supplied 80 per cent of the world's coal. The coalfields stretched from Scotland to Somerset but were mostly in the central part of the country. The coal had to be cut out of the ground by hand. It was then carried in baskets or pulled along in wheeled tubs that ran on railway tracks.

Most of the miners were men, but many women and children also worked down the mine. Many of these children were between five and nine years old. They were often beaten if they did not work hard enough.

The coal was cut from the ground by the men and boys. It was then carried along dark passages by pit ponies or pushed in carts on rails. In some of the smaller mines, women and girls called 'drawers' had to pull the heavy coal baskets behind them on their hands and knees. In other mines, female 'bearers' had to carry the coal on their backs up steep slopes, stairways or ladders to the surface. Bearers often worked for ten hours or more without a break.

Victorian Reforms

Gradually <u>reforms</u> were made to improve the lives of the workers in factories and mines. The government passed laws to limit the working day to ten hours for women and children. Factory Acts made new rules for guarding dangerous machinery. In 1842 the Mines Act became law, stopping children under ten years old working in the coal mines. Conditions for workers did improve by the end of Victoria's reign although some factory owners ignored the new laws.

Children at work

Parents who worked in the factories did not earn much money. They had to send their children out to work in order to earn enough money to feed the family. The owners of the factories liked to employ children because they could pay them less. Boys and girls as young as five worked in the factories and mines. Sometimes they had to work for 12 hours a day.

We sweep 78 chimneys in three days.

We were sold for £1 and 10 shillings.

▲ *Many children had to work on the streets. This boy cleaned people's shoes.*

▲ *These children are working in the brickyards where they have to carry large lumps of clay for the brick makers.*

Climbing boys

Victorian towns had plenty of sooty chimneys to keep chimney sweeps busy. Some chimney sweeps used boys who clambered up inside the chimneys to knock the soot down. Sometimes the sweeps stuck pins in the boys' feet to make them climb faster. Climbing boys were always black with soot and many never had a good wash. Many died of lung diseases while they were still young.

Victorian Reforms

In 1842 the Mines Act stopped children under ten working in the mines. In 1843 children under ten were stopped from working as sweeps. This made very poor families even worse off. Many lied about their children's ages to employers. In 1875 the use of climbing boys was stopped altogether.

Children at school

▲ *This is a picture of a ragged school. Here, children were taught the basics of reading, writing and mental arithmetic. They learnt the Bible as well.*

Poor children

In early Victorian Britain many children never went to school at all. Parents had to pay for their children to go to school, but some families were too poor to afford education. They sent their children out to work in the factories instead.

Some children went to schools run by the churches. These church schools had one large classroom that might have as many as 100 pupils in it. One teacher sat at the front of the class. Older pupils called monitors or pupil teachers helped teach the younger children.

If there were no church schools children might be sent to a dame school. Here old ladies would use their parlour as a small schoolroom. Many children were so poor that they could only attend charity schools called ragged schools. Here children were taught and also trained to work in an industry.

From 1862 the government gave money to the church schools. This meant they could keep down the costs for parents. To earn this money the children were tested in the three Rs, **R**eading, w**R**iting and a**R**ithmetic. These tests were very unpopular with teachers and pupils.

Rich children

Middle-class parents sent their boys to the local grammar school. Here they spent a lot of time learning Greek and Latin grammar.

Richer families employed a tutor to teach their sons at home. When the boys were older they were sent away to a public school to become a 'complete gentleman'.

Wealthy Victorians thought that girls should be educated differently from boys. Their education was supposed to train them to become good wives. It would include sketching, playing the piano, singing, sewing and perhaps skills like deportment. Rich families employed a governess who lived with the family and educated their daughters.

▲ *This shows an art class at a Victorian school.*

▼ *Picture of a Victorian dame's school by Thomas Webster.*

Victorian Reforms

Many people wanted all children to have a good education. In 1870 the Education Act was passed. Boards of Education were set up to provide schooling in every area. A number of new schools were built called Board Schools. They were often ugly buildings, more like an army barracks or a prison than schools now. Children sat in rows in large, mixed-age classes.

The Education Act of 1880 said that all children between five and ten had to go to school. Even then many poor families kept their children away from school and sent them to the factories to earn money. It was only in 1918, after Victoria's reign, that a law was passed to stop any child under 12 years working for a living.

Toys

Children in Victorian times had no televisions, personal stereos, video or computer games. However, rich children did have lots of beautiful toys to play with.

In the nursery

In most nurseries the favourite toy was the wooden rocking horse. Rocking horses were always brightly painted, with a mane of real horse's hair.

Another nursery favourite was the dolls' house. Lots of furniture could be bought for the house, as well as lamps, ornaments and even small books.

▲ *A very large and elaborate Victorian dolls' house.*

▲ *This is a Victorian rocking horse. Unfortunately, over the years it has lost its mane.*

Dolls

The Victorians were very good at making beautiful dolls. The head was usually made of wax or china. The body was made of cloth or wood. Even poor children would have had dolls, usually made from wood, or perhaps just a simple wooden spoon or washing peg wrapped in cloth. Rich children's dolls were dressed in fabulous clothes made out of expensive materials.

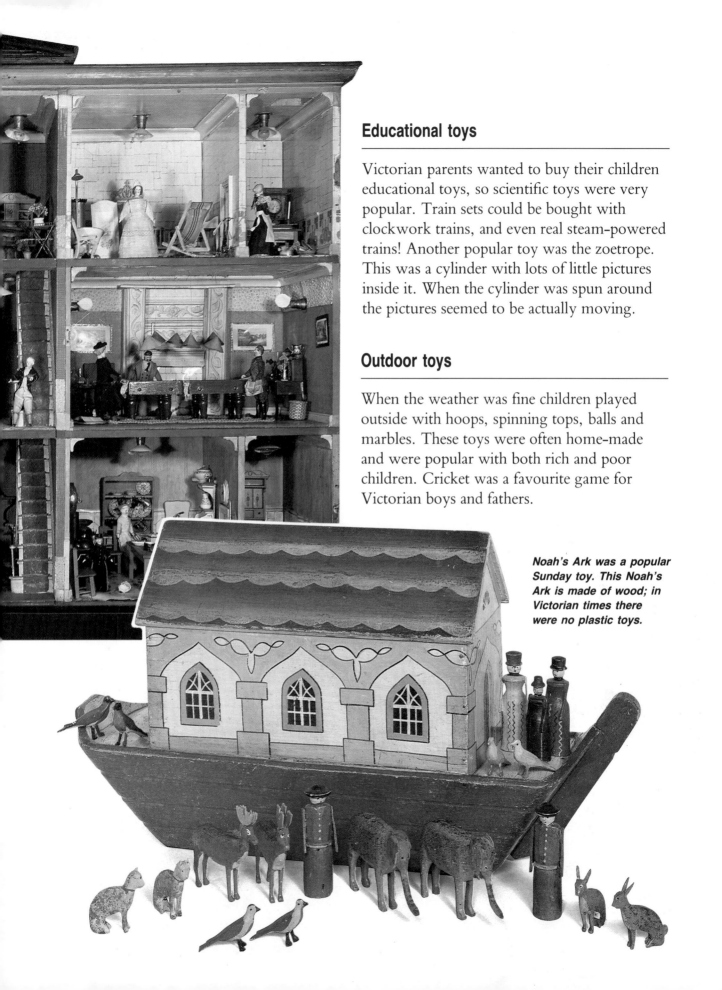

Educational toys

Victorian parents wanted to buy their children educational toys, so scientific toys were very popular. Train sets could be bought with clockwork trains, and even real steam-powered trains! Another popular toy was the zoetrope. This was a cylinder with lots of little pictures inside it. When the cylinder was spun around the pictures seemed to be actually moving.

Outdoor toys

When the weather was fine children played outside with hoops, spinning tops, balls and marbles. These toys were often home-made and were popular with both rich and poor children. Cricket was a favourite game for Victorian boys and fathers.

Noah's Ark was a popular Sunday toy. This Noah's Ark is made of wood; in Victorian times there were no plastic toys.

Country life

Most land in the country was owned by rich people whom we call the landed gentry. They lived in large houses in the countryside or in villages. Poor people could not afford to buy much land. They had to work as farm labourers for the landed gentry but were paid very badly. Many poor people left the countryside and moved to the towns to find work in the factories or mines.

Villages

Most villages in the country had a number of craftspeople in them like the blacksmith, the wheelwright, the carpenter, the miller, the saddler and the shoemaker. There would also be a vicar and perhaps a schoolmaster. Most villages had a number of public houses where labourers would gather and drink.

A labourer's cottage

Labourers' cottages were built of stone with thatched roofs. They were often very small, damp and crumbling. Several people in the family would share a single bedroom or even a bed. These cottages were usually owned by the farmer. If the labourers lost their jobs they would also lose their homes. Most labourers also had a small piece of land on which they could grow some of their own food.

◄ *Working in the fields was as hard as working in the factories and mines, but at least it was not as dangerous. This photograph was taken during the harvest in 1880.*

▼ *Painting of a Victorian harvest scene.*

Working on the land

At harvest time almost everybody, men, women and children, helped collect the corn. This meant that schools had to close and give their pupils a holiday! The corn had to be cut with scythes, gathered together in bundles, and carried on horse-drawn carts to the barn. It had to be threshed by hand to separate the grain from the chaff.

Farm work was very hard. There were no tractors or combine harvesters. To plough a field a farmer had to steer a horse-drawn plough by hand. During Victoria's reign tools like the scythe were better made and so the work became a little easier. Farmers began to use steam-powered machines to thresh the grain. By the 1870s a quarter of grain harvesting was done by machinery. These new machines made life easier, but they also put some people out of work.

Depression

During the 1870s there were a number of very poor harvests. At the same time cheap food came into Britain from Australia and the United States of America. Even more people left the countryside in search of work.

This is what a Victorian labourer's cottage may have looked like inside. You can see it is very crowded, with poor lighting and no drains. Water had to be collected from a pump outside.

Victorian women

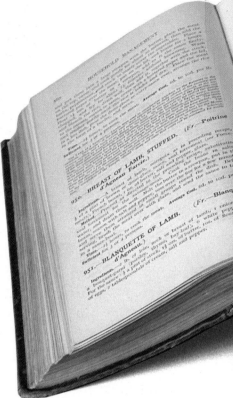

◀ *Many women worked in factories. By the end of the century factories were usually clean and the work was not as hard as in early Victorian times.*

Wealthy women were not expected to go out to work. Their job was to stay at home and look after the house. They were responsible for organising the servants and seeing that the children were brought up correctly.

Only a few women were rich enough to live like this. Most had to work much harder. They had full-time jobs and were often responsible for the housework as well. They were not usually paid as well as men.

Many women worked as servants to the middle and upper classes. They would clean and cook and help their mistress to dress. Some servants looked after the children. Well-educated women were often employed as governesses.

Poor women worked in coal mines, in factories, in mills, and in the fields. They also worked in laundries, shops and sweatshops to make cheap clothes.

◀ In 1861 this famous book was published to help middle-class women run their homes. Mrs Beeton's book gave advice on almost anything that was needed to run a household.

A woman's place?

Many Victorian men thought that women were inferior to them. Women were not allowed to vote in elections, to own property, or to have the same sort of education as men. Wealthy Victorian men thought that a woman's place was in the home. They did not want their wives to go out to work; but they did not mind employing women as servants.

During Victoria's reign some women tried to make things fairer. In 1848, the first college for women was opened in London. Two students of this college, Miss Buss and Miss Beale, went on to found schools for girls. Lydia Becker tried to get the vote for women, but even Queen Victoria herself did not think women should vote.

▲ Advertisement for Victorian women's clothes.

Inventions and discoveries

The Victorian period was an age of many inventions and discoveries. Most people used oil lamps and candles to light their homes. During Victoria's reign wealthier people began to use gas to heat and light their homes and towns. They also used steam power to run huge machines in their factories and in their fields in the countryside.

Then, thanks to the work of scientists like Faraday, Edison and Swann, electricity was discovered and used. (You can read more about the way steam and electricity were used for trains on page 33.) The grimy cities became brighter places as electricity replaced the old gas lamps to give lighter and safer streets.

▼ *Advertisement for one of the first Victorian washing machines. Families who bought the latest washing machines would not have to employ a 'washerwoman' to do their washing.*

► *An early Victorian telephone. Being able to talk over long distances must have helped Victorian businessmen.*

Refrigerators, typewriters, gramophones, cameras and cinemas were all Victorian inventions. They soon became part of the everyday lives of wealthier families. Poorer people could only marvel at these new inventions. If they worked as servants in large households some inventions, like the washing machine, actually helped. Some people were put out of work by the new inventions but these inventions also created employment.

Communications

Communications were greatly improved as well. In 1841 the first national postal service was introduced. Letters could be sent for a penny. The telegraph system of sending messages was established and the cable linking England to the United States was finished in 1858. The telegraph system was soon replaced by the telephone and by wireless telegraphy (radio). By the end of the Victorian age in 1901 radio signals had been sent across the Atlantic from Cornwall to Newfoundland in Canada.

▲ *Portrait of Charles Darwin, a great Victorian scientist.*

▲ *The Great Exhibition opened in 1851.*

Prince Albert

Victoria's husband Prince Albert took a great interest in British affairs, science and technology, and in working conditions. He planned a huge exhibition to be held in an enormous glass building called the Crystal Palace. The Great Exhibition opened in 1851 and was visited by over six million people. People travelled from all around the world to see the amazing Victorian inventions and engines, and over 1,000 products like clothes, textiles and furniture.

Darwin

Perhaps the single piece of scientific work that created the biggest sensation was Charles Darwin's book on the *Origin of Species*. In this book, Darwin challenged the idea of creation, taught by the Church, and put forward his theory of evolution.

Before Darwin, many people had believed that all animals were created by God on the same day. Darwin proved that this was not true. He argued that animals are constantly changing and evolving; one species slowly evolving into a new species. He claimed that humans had evolved from apes. Many people disagreed with Darwin, but his new ideas totally changed the way we look at animals and at human history.

Travel and transport

Travel by road

At the beginning of the Victorian period most people in the towns simply walked to their work or to the shops. Wealthier people had their own carriage or could hire a 'hansom cab'. In the country the horse was used more.

Journeys between towns soon became much quicker than they had previously been, thanks to the improved roads and coaching system. In and between each town were coaching inns where passengers could rest and get refreshments and where horses could be changed. The railways also helped people travel between towns (see pages 32 and 33).

For short distances and daily trips across the town, horse-drawn buses soon became popular. By 1850, buses had a bench seat across the top so that about ten people could sit back-to-back outside as well as having 12 people inside. They had a driver and a conductor.

Fares were still high so it was not until the introduction of the electric tram at the end of the 19th century that the working people could do anything other than walk to work.

▼ *Life on the canals in Victorian times.*

1

Travel by water

Heavy goods were carried by sea in ships or on rivers and canals by barges. The canals made it much cheaper for industry to move materials around the country. Before Victoria's reign a network of inland waterways had been built up across the country linking all the main industrial centres.

We wrapped ourselves more closely in our coats and [p]repared with many half suppressed moans to encounter the piercing blast which swept across the open country.

▲ *The penny-farthing was a popular form of transport in the 1870s.*

Pedal power

During the 1870s the penny-farthing bicycle was introduced. It was uncomfortable and dangerous to ride. By 1886 a 'safety bicycle' was on sale, similar to the bicycles we use today. At the turn of the century the car was invented, and used as a means of transport for the wealthy.

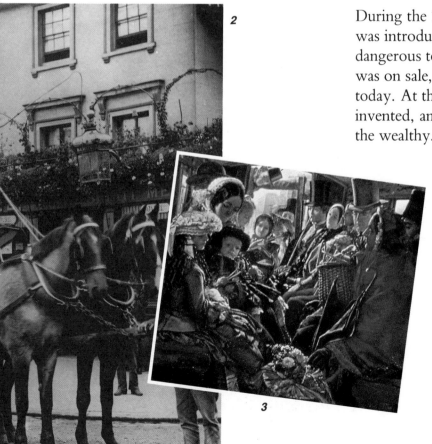

1. This horse-bus is in the London Transport Museum. In this photograph, the horse-bus has been taken out of the Museum for a trip.

2. This horse-drawn bus was used by Victorian people to travel across London. It has a bench seat across the top and seats inside.

3. This painting shows what it may have been like travelling in a Victorian horse-drawn bus.

The railways

The railways were a source of great pride to the Victorians. They also dramatically changed everyday life as they became a major form of transport for both people and goods. Just before Victoria became queen, the first modern passenger railway was opened between Liverpool and Manchester. Before then, railways had been used mainly to take coal from the mines to the factories or canals.

Spread of the railways

The railways spread rapidly as they provided a quick and cheap means of transport. By the 1850s most of the main parts of England, Scotland and Wales were joined by the railways. Engineers like Isambard Kingdom Brunel planned great bridges and other engineering marvels to enable the trains to run across all sorts of rivers, marshes, through hills and over deep valleys.

◄ Constructing the Metropolitan Railway through Paddington in the 1860s.

▼ Miners at work constructing an underground railway tunnel.

The Underground

As London became more crowded its roads became congested. From 1862 onwards underground railways were opened. Travelling on the new London Underground was unpleasant with all the smoke billowing along the long dark tunnels; but in 1890 electric trains replaced the steam ones.

◄ Metropolitan Railway steam train, built in 1866. The large pipe on the side of the train reduced the amount of steam and smoke that was emitted into the tunnel.

Effects of the railways

The railways had an effect on many aspects of life. Some of these were better than others:

• Communications were greatly improved as a fast system of carrying the mail was quickly established.

• People from around the country who shared common interests could meet each other. National organisations like trade unions could link up with their local groups.

• Special events like the Great Exhibition could be visited by people from all over the country.

• Commuters could travel into the towns and cities to work.

• Fresh food could be carried from the farms into the cities quickly.

• Many new jobs were created for the railway builders (called navvies), as well as all the people who operated the railway.

• Complaints were made about the smoke and pollution, and about animals being frightened.

• People who worked on the canals or for coaching companies lost their jobs as their work was taken over by the railways.

• People from the smoky towns were able to go on holiday to seaside resorts.

Victorian medicine

Today most people can expect to live beyond their 70th birthday. Food and water is usually safe and clean, we are vaccinated against most major diseases, and if we do get sick we are usually quickly cured by our doctors. At the beginning of Queen Victoria's reign things were very different. Food and water were often dirty and contained germs. Doctors charged fees to treat patients, so poor people often had to go to filthy 'free hospitals'. Most people died before they had even reached their 40th birthday.

▲ *A group of Victorian nurses.*

◄ *Cartoon of the diseases that existed in the River Thames during Victorian times.*

▼ *Drawing showing Lister's carbolic spray being used in an operation. The introduction of antiseptics made operations safer.*

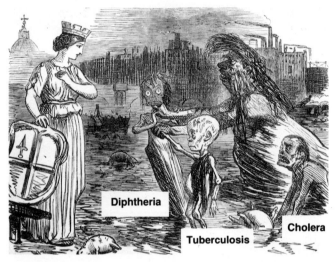

Diphtheria

Tuberculosis

Cholera

Cholera

In our country today, diseases like cholera, tuberculosis and typhoid have been eliminated or controlled. But in Victorian times terrible diseases like cholera were carried in dirty food and water. Cholera epidemics were so bad that in 1848 Parliament passed a Public Health Act and set up a Board of Health to attempt to fight it. It was not until 1855 that the Victorians discovered the cause of cholera and began to try to get cleaner water supplies. By 1900 every town had a Medical Officer of Health, main drainage, a proper rubbish collection service and an organised water system.

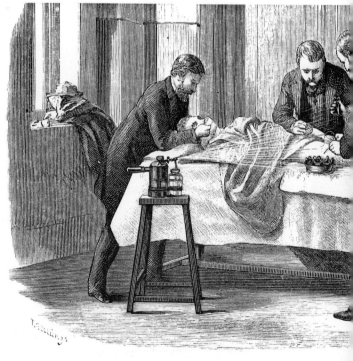

Doctors and hospitals

At the beginning of Victoria's reign, doctors still believed that putting blood-sucking leeches onto sick people, or putting red-hot irons onto wounds cured people. Doctors were better trained as the century progressed but patients who consulted a doctor still had to pay.

Victorian hospitals often made their patients worse rather than better. Doctors and nurses did not realise that cleanliness and hygiene stopped the spread of germs and disease. Doctors performed operations wearing their normal clothes and without sterilising the instruments!

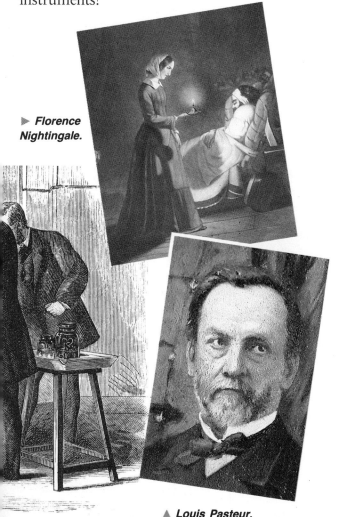

▶ **Florence Nightingale.**

▲ **Louis Pasteur.**

Hospitals did improve during Victoria's reign, thanks to the work of Florence Nightingale and Mary Seacole. These two women worked as nurses during the Crimean War. Wounded soldiers usually died from diseases they had caught in hospital. Florence and Mary showed that with good food, clean conditions, and proper care and attention many soldiers could be cured. After the war Florence Nightingale continued to train nurses and improve hospitals. The Victorians thought both women were heroines, but they soon forgot about Mary Seacole.

New discoveries

In Victorian times, operations were carried out without any anaesthetics (painkillers) or antiseptics (germ-killing disinfectants). The poor patients often died from shock during the operation, or from infections afterwards. But some important new discoveries changed Victorian medicine.

In 1847 a Scottish doctor, James Simpson, used a liquid called chloroform as an anaesthetic during an operation. Chloroform made the patient remain unconscious (in a deep sleep) during the operation, with no harmful after-effects.

Scientists like Louis Pasteur had discovered that wounds became infected because of invisible germs and bacteria. In 1865 Joseph Lister successfully used an antiseptic spray to kill off germs during an operation. Doctors also discovered how to vaccinate against killer diseases like smallpox.

Despite these advances, by the end of Victoria's reign average life expectancy was still only 46. Even Prince Albert died of typhoid fever when he was only 42.

Art and literature

Bob Cratchit went down a slide on Cornhill, at the end of a lane of boys, twenty times, in honour of its being Christmas Eve

▲ *Painting of the British countryside by William Turner.*

◀ *Illustration by a famous Victorian artist, Arthur Rackham, from* A Christmas Carol *by Charles Dickens.*

▶ *These William Morris designs were very popular in Victorian times.*

Writers for children

You may already have heard or read stories by Victorian writers. Charles Dickens wrote a number of books including *A Christmas Carol, Oliver Twist* and *David Copperfield*. Frances Hodgson Burnett wrote many stories including *The Secret Garden*. In 1865 Lewis Carroll wrote *Alice's Adventures in Wonderland*.

Writers and poets

There was no television or radio in Victorian times. Poetry readings were one popular form of entertainment. One of the most famous Victorian poets is Alfred, Lord Tennyson, whose work was greatly appreciated by Victorians.

Art

William Turner was a very successful artist whose work aroused great interest. His work helped Victorians to remember the power of nature. There were many other great artists from the rest of Europe. All middle- and upper-class homes would have a number of paintings around the house.

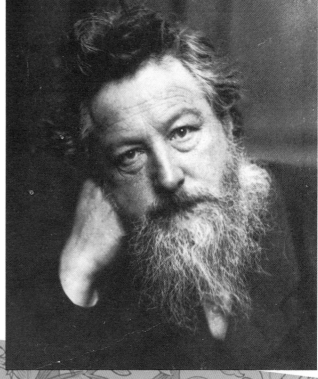

▶ *William Morris.*

Decorating the home

William Morris had an enormous effect on the way rich Victorians decorated their houses. Morris produced his own designs for furniture, carpets, curtains and wallpaper. He also manufactured his designs. Even today many people still buy wallpaper and furnishings decorated with William Morris patterns.

37

Entertainment and leisure

Many working people spent much of their leisure time in the local public house. During Victorian times more time was allowed off work for feast days and church events. Shorter working days also helped provide more opportunity for leisure.

▼ *Tennis was popular amongst the upper-classes. Women played tennis wearing long skirts and long-sleeved blouses.*

PUNCH·AND·JUDY

HAVE you a penny? well then, stay!
Haven't you any? don't go away!
Punch holds receptions all through the day,
Squeaking aloud to gather a crowd,
Scolding at Toby, beating his Wife,
Frightening the Constable out of his life,
And making jokes in a terrible passion,
As is Mr. Punch's peculiar fashion;
For this is his old, delightful plan
Of getting as many pence as he can.
Then away he'll jog,
With his Wife and his Dog,
New folks to meet
In the very next street.

Sport

During Victorian times there was a growing interest in sport which was seen as a healthy outdoor activity. Football, cricket, boxing and horse racing all attracted large crowds. For the middle and upper classes the range of sports was greater. There were golf, tennis, croquet, archery and horse riding. Towards the end of the century cycling also became popular.

Entertainment

The streets of the towns and cities were crowded places where street entertainers such as jugglers, comedians, acrobats, musicians and even fire-eaters made a living.

From about 1850 onwards music halls became popular. Here singers, comedians and other entertainers could perform and be watched in a theatre. By the end of the century some music hall performers like Marie Lloyd were as famous as modern pop stars. Technology also helped provide a new entertainment at the end of the century. Cinemas were set up in local halls for one or two nights to show black-and-white moving pictures – but there was no sound.

▲ *Victorians at the seaside. People changed into their bathing costumes in the bathing huts, which were then wheeled into the sea.*

◄ *Punch and Judy shows were popular entertainment in Victorian times.*

Holidays

Rich Victorians had always been able to afford holidays in Europe. Seaside holidays in England soon became more popular. Children could play in the sand or paddle in the sea while adults could sit in the sun, or bathe in the chilly sea.

Thanks to the cheap transport provided by the railways, poorer people could also afford trips to the sea. Many seaside towns such as Blackpool became famous as holiday resorts. The larger resorts had theatres, amusement parks, piers, promenades, zoos and bandstands.

Religion and the Victorian Sunday

Going to church

Nearly all the middle and upper classes went to church on Sunday and so did some of the working classes. The different church groups did not always get on well with each other but there was a feeling that most Victorian families were 'God-fearing'. In many families, the father would gather the family together, often including the servants, and say prayers. Victorians are often said to have valued the Bible and the idea of hard work.

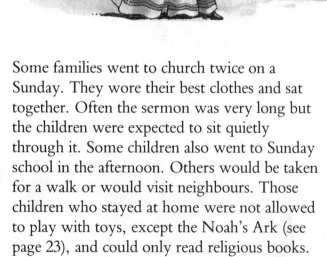

My back still aches when I remember those long services.

▲ Painting by a Victorian artist, Millais, of a child asleep during a sermon.

Some families went to church twice on a Sunday. They wore their best clothes and sat together. Often the sermon was very long but the children were expected to sit quietly through it. Some children also went to Sunday school in the afternoon. Others would be taken for a walk or would visit neighbours. Those children who stayed at home were not allowed to play with toys, except the Noah's Ark (see page 23), and could only read religious books.

Keeping Sunday for God

In the later part of Victoria's reign there were strict rules about what people were allowed to do on a Sunday. No one was allowed to work, unless the work was essential or for charity. All shops and public places like museums were closed, people were not allowed to play sports and there were no other amusements.

Christmas

Victorians thought it was important to be charitable at Christmas. Charles Dickens' story *A Christmas Carol* (see page 35) is all about being kind and generous at Christmas.

At Christmas it was traditional for wealthy people to give useful items to their servants. Victorian children got Christmas stockings filled with fruit and nuts, and perhaps a toy or two and a book.

Many of our Christmas traditions started in Victorian England. Prince Albert introduced the Christmas tree from Germany in 1848. The Victorians also liked singing carols, decorating their houses with holly and mistletoe, going to a pantomime, and pulling Christmas crackers.

◄ *An illustration from a Victorian Christmas card.*

▼ *Victorian shops were closed on Sundays. People still argue today about whether shops should open on Sunday.*

▼ *'Stirring the Christmas pudding' from a picture by Henry Woods.*

Government, law and punishment

Although Victoria was the queen, the country was governed by Parliament. The two most famous Victorian prime ministers were Benjamin Disraeli, a Tory, and William Gladstone, a Liberal. Both men wanted to make changes to improve education and help the poor.

▲ *This cartoon, drawn in 1867, illustrates that Parliament did not want to allow working-class men to vote. However, in 1884 all men were allowed to vote.*

The right to vote

When Victoria came to the throne only rich men who owned land or factories were allowed to vote. It was not until 1867 that all men living in towns had the right to vote at elections. But voting was not done in secret – everyone could see who you were voting for. Rich candidates might try to bribe or bully people to vote for them. In 1872 voting was finally made secret, as it is today.

The councils that ran the towns were also elected more fairly. The same rights were given to men in the country in 1884. Women did not have the right to vote at all.

The police

The police force had been started about eight years before Victoria became queen. The force was started by Robert Peel, so the police were often called 'peelers' or 'bobbies'. The use of a police force to keep law and order in the towns quickly spread. At first the police were not liked, even by law-abiding people. But as the years went on, and they began to reduce crime, they became more popular.

▲ *Police officers in Victorian times.*

In Victorian times voting was very different from today. Women were not allowed to vote, and voting did not take place in secret until 1872.

Crime and punishment

The law was harsh. Floggings could be ordered for quite minor offences. Up to 1878, children of five and six were still sent to adult prisons. For some of them it was better than living on the streets! Stealing could even result in deportation to Australia.

Until 1868 hangings were still carried out in public and were watched by huge crowds. Overnight, people would gather in the streets outside the prison to get a good view. People whose windows overlooked the scaffold would charge spectators for a good view.

I was whipped twice for thieving and had been to prison five times.

The British Empire

THE BRITISH EMPIRE

Building an empire

During Victoria's reign Britain ruled many parts of the world. Many Victorians left Britain to settle in other countries. Sometimes they simply wanted to begin a new life, in countries like Australia, New Zealand and Canada.

Sometimes the British were like invaders, seizing land and power in places like India and Africa which they added to the British Empire. The Victorians thought that the people of these countries were inferior to them. Local rulers and customs were ignored and replaced by British governors and laws. Britain had a strong army and navy which it used to force these people to obey.

A map of the British Empire in 1900. By the end of Victoria's reign Britain controlled a large part of the world.

POINTS OF VIEW

Many Victorians believed that they were helping the people of the countries they invaded by bringing them European customs and government.
Do you think they were right?

44

India

The heart of the British Empire was India. In the 18th and 19th centuries people from Britain went to India to make money. They sold Indian tea, silk and cotton to other countries and became very rich. Many of the colonists looked down on the Indians as an inferior people and expected them to accept British laws and ways of life. A large army was kept in India to enforce British law for many years.

Sometimes force had to be used to keep the Indians under control. In 1857 the Indians objected to the rules they had to live under and some of the Indian soldiers in the British army mutinied. The mutiny was quickly put down, but the Indian people still wanted to be free of British rule.

The scramble for Africa

Victorian missionaries and explorers like David Livingstone found out a lot about Africa. The countries of Europe saw Africa as a new area for empire building. By 1900 much of it had been divided up between them. Countries such as Britain, Belgium, France and Germany raced each other to get new territories with very little thought for the people who lived there. They used their armies to defeat African chiefs and their warriors. From its African colonies, Britain was supplied with cocoa, coffee, teak, mahogany and diamonds.

Why did people want an empire?

Ordinary people wanted to make a fresh start, with the chance to establish a business of their own.

Traders and industrialists wanted to open up new markets for their goods. Investors and bankers wanted to invest money to make large profits.

Some politicians wanted to stop other European countries from having their own powerful empires.

Some wanted to convert more people to Christianity.

Victorian heritage

It is not difficult to find out more about the Victorians; there is evidence all around us. Old maps, census returns and street directories may tell you about Victorians that lived in your area. You may also find some signs like these near you.

▲ *Some houses even have the date when they were built on them.*

◄ *This house was built in Victorian times for a wealthy family. It is now divided into flats. Look in your local area and see if you can find any Victorian houses. See if you can spot any change that have been made to them.*

▼ *In some towns the roads have been named after famous Victorian people. Look at a local map and see what names you can recognise. Do you think the houses in those streets were built during, before, or after Victorian times?*

◄ *This plate was made to celebrate Queen Victoria's Diamond Jubilee.*

▼ *There are many old photographs of towns in Victorian times. Your local library may have some that you can borrow, buy or copy. See if you can match an old photograph to a modern place near you.*

▲ *Many museums contain artefacts that tell us a lot about life in Victorian times. This is the Victoria and Albert Museum in London.*

Glossary

These words are underlined in this book.

Deportation
To be sent away from one country to another, as a punishment.

Deportment
Learning manners.

Empire
A group of countries that are ruled by the same authority, for example by a queen or an emperor.

Governess
A woman who is employed to teach children in a private, wealthy household.

Great Exhibition
An exhibition of Victorian inventions, engines and new products held at Crystal Palace in 1851.

Inferior
Something or someone of a lower position. In Victorian times, women were seen as inferior to men.

Influence
The effect that a person or thing has on another.

Landed gentry
People who own land, or have inherited it, and are therefore very rich.

Middle class
A group of people within society that falls between the upper and lower classes.

Nanny
A person who is employed to be a child's nurse.

Ragged schools
Victorian schools that were funded by charity, to educate poor children, and give them an industrial training.

Reconstruction
Building or restoring something so that it appears as it was originally.

Reform
To make something better, by removing the faults and errors in it. In Victorian times many laws were reformed.

Sweatshops
A workshop where people had to work very hard.

Telegraph
A system for transmitting messages or signals, by using electricity.

Textile mill
A factory where cloth or fabric is made.

Vaccinate
To give people a small dose of medicine in order to protect them against a disease.

Workhouse
A place where poor, able-bodied people worked in return for food and accommodation.